Thank you for buying this book. As a former starting quarterback at BYU, I've been asked on multiple occasions if I could teach boys and young men how to play quarterback. Questions like, "Hey, do you think you could spend an hour with my boy at the park and teach him some basics?" come up often in conversations.

As a coach and teacher, I figured; why not give some basic fundamentals that anyone can use? From little league to the highest levels of QB play, these drills and skills are the building blocks of fundamental quarterback play. Practice these skills until your toes hurt!

It's my goal that the information provided in this book will give you some valuable insights on quarterback play and will help you perform to the highest level your body and mind will allow you to go!

If the fundamental skills that are written about in this book are applied, your quarterback **WILL BE** successful.

Give this easy to use book to your student of the game and watch his game flourish! The sky truly is the limit.

To future success,
Charlie Peterson

Table of Contents

What is a quarterback anyway?

Being a quarterback is a full time job. It requires 100% concentration and a total commitment far greater than any other position on the football field.

A quarterback is thrown into a leadership role and must be willing and able to handle all the stress that goes with such a position. After all, the QB touches the ball every single snap! Nobody, not the running back, not the receiver, not the offensive lineman has as much mental burden placed on them as the quarterback.

Teammates and coaches look up to the quarterback for guidance all the time, not just in games of on the football field. A strong QB realizes that he is in the spotlight regardless of where he is or what he is doing.

The QB is the one individual who must set the example and be the leader of his football team. The best quarterbacks take ownership of their play. If you're a strong quarterback, your teammates are going to follow you and your leaderships regardless of whether it is good or bad… and a QB must always lead his team in a positive manner. ALWAYS.

If you are willing to accept the challenge of being the "example setter" and wanting to make you and your teammates better – you are on the road of becoming a dominant QB and leader.

A quarterback is the CEO, the President, the Principal of the football organization. The offensive team is beholden to him and his talents. A whole football team can be made or broken by the decisions the quarterback makes.

The QB is not only responsible for his own play, but he has to be mentally capable and alert enough to understand what each player on his offense is supposed to do. Then, he has to be astute enough to understand what each player on the defense is responsible for also! Great QB's understand all 22 positions on the football field. That's a tremendous amount of information to grasp…. and it's extremely difficult. That is why only the CREAM of the CROP plays quarterback.

If you are someone who wants to lead and showcase skills for a whole team to follow – the quarterback position is the one for you!

The Development of a Quarterback

Talent   **Knowledge**   **Time**   **Dedication**

The QB is the most important man on the football team. The team will never be any stronger than its QB. The team with a superb QB will be a fighting team with confidence and fierce pride: a smart team with high morale; a team that is on edge, will finish strong and win the close games. The superb QB leads his team to victory in the crucial game.

A QUARTERBACK MUST ACCEPT 2 FACTS THAT GO WITH THE MOST IMPORTANT POSITION OF ANY TEAM SPORT:

1: He will be subject to more second-guessing and criticism than any other player or coach.

2: Knowledge, self-discipline and concentration lead to consistency. Only careful and sound preparation will produce the results to develop into a championship QB.

THE PURPOSE OF THIS BOOK IS THREEFOLD

A -To assist you in your preparation for the coming season.

B - To broaden your knowledge of offensive plans and opponents defenses

C - To strengthen the link of communication and understanding between the QB's and coaches and QB's and players.

Coach   QB   Player Relationship

There must be an atmosphere of mutual trust and confidence between the QB and coaches at all times. Willingness to understand, communicate freely and discuss ideas on a personal level must prevail; recognize and respect the job responsibility of each other.

The QB must serve as the golden link in the chain of communication between the coaches and the team. It is here the QB must play a major role. He must function with such a workable knowledge of what the coaches are striving for that he will trigger a positive response from the team and produce outstanding results.

Qualities of a Quarterback

A QB should have superior qualities of voice, enunciation, bearing, intelligence and understanding. He must be dedicated, consistent, persevering, a positive thinker, be willing to sacrifice, be self-disciplined, have an eagerness to acquire knowledge and a strong desire to master the mechanics of the game.

Outward Confidence Inner Commitment

Dynamic Leadership will be his Greatest Asset

The Quarterback as a Leader

Any successful organization can only continue to function as it receives direction and leadership from the top. The smoother it runs, the better the leadership and direction. Men are not born leaders. Leadership is not a mantle somebody places on one's shoulders. Leadership is acquired through continuous effort and attention to detail.

The outstanding quarterback is the leader of the offensive team. Other players depend upon him for direction. He becomes successful only if he is willing to give his attention and energy to detail, and to work every day to give himself the background and ability to perform his duties.

The morale of a team largely depends upon the Quarterback's ability to lift and direct them. If the quarterback is an individual with high morale, with determination and a will to win, the team will respond accordingly.

** 1 – THE SPIRITUAL QUALITY **

A – The spirit and morale of a football team originate from its quarterback.

I- This does not mean being a "pop off" or leading cheers.

II- It means going about daily work in a cheerful, vigorous, aggressive manner.

III- This quality can be developed through practice.

IV- This quality becomes easier to those who possess fine attitudes toward teammates and coaches.

B- Poise is a trait that sticks out all over a quarterback.

I- You hear it in his voice.

II- You note it in his bearing.

III- You sense it in his manner.

IV- His every action expresses to his teammates and opponents that he knows exactly what he will do next.

C- A Quarterback is quietly confident at all times and continuously works to gain the confidence of others.

I- This does not mean being a braggart.

II-   Never be hasty to voice opinions on matters involving teammates. One can gain respect by having the right answer rather than by jumping to conclusions.

III-   If you cannot speak highly of a teammate, refrain from saying anything.

IV-   Respect can be gained through sincerity.

"The test of leadership is whether on has the ability to keep his head while others are losing theirs." – Kipling

D – The QB MUST be able to CONCENTRATE.

I-   The Great QB's have the ability to concentrate to the point of "losing themselves" in the ball game.

II-   The one and only objective is to win.
    a. Never lose sight of this objective.
    b. Practice the habit of winning.
    c. The "desire to win" is not the "will" to win. Everybody has the desire, only some have the will.

III - The great QB does not approach the game in a blind, frenzied manner; rather he is cool and calculating.
    a. He is ready to capitalize on opponent's mistakes.
    b. If the opponent does not make mistakes voluntarily, the good QB forces his hand onto the opponent.

IV -   If you will be great, you must first
lose yourself in your team.

E – Boundless ambition and determination are
necessary for success in Quarterbacking.
        I – Great quarterback play does NOT come
easy… if it did, everybody would play QB!

F- Resourcefulness

        I – Many quarterbacks would be great if
they had this quality.
        II – Have faith in yourself and your
teammates.
        III – The resourceful Quarterback is able to
counter at all times. He pulls the unexpected
without gambling. He turns opponent's mistakes
into touchdowns.
        IV – One can become resourceful only by
being alert in practice for the opportunity to practice
the art.

LEADERSHIP CAN BE CREATED
TAKE CHARGE   KEEP CONTROL

2. ** THE MENTAL QUALITY **

a. Learn to make the correct decision quickly

b. Learn to analyze and catalogue details under pressure and competition.

c. Know when to take a chance and when not to.

d. Develop your imagination by mental imagery off the field in your spare time.

e. Learn to keep your mind on your objective regardless of the score. (And what is the objective? The objective is to WIN!)

f. Foresight which springs from the mind and experience, must be acquired. Many QB's know what the trend of the game will be soon after it commences, and can plan their attack accordingly.

g. Develop the ability to think clearly under pressure.

h. After you have quarterbacked a team in practice or in a game, you should go back over each play carefully, examine your strategy relative to the opponent, your team, and the defense. Did you make the correct decisions?

i. Know the offensive and defensive strategy.

3. ** THE PHYSICAL QUALITY **

Since the team depends upon you, be at your best physically. You cannot be alert mentally, or be able to carry the load spiritually, if you do not get the proper rest. Most great men, who depend on their minds, realize that mental alertness is related to physical well-being. The mind can only be alert if the body gets the proper rest, diet and nutrition. Nine hours sleep each night should be a minimum during fall practice. You cannot dissipate your energies and have a clear, alert mind. Good conditioning comes from work, diet, and rest in proper proportions. Learn to know yourself. It is important that you distribute your meals throughout the day; breakfast should be a heavy meal, lunch before practice should be light, your stomach should be empty when you come on the practice field and dinner should be heavy. You must be able to give your best effort at all times. YOU ARE THE LEADER!

4. ** THE MECHANICAL QUALITY **

A: No other position in sports demands such rigid conformity to the basic fundamentals. Learn to work diligently, to perfect yourself in the mechanics of quarterback play. Make sure you come off the practice field better than when you went on. Examine your mistakes... do not repeat them.

Greatness in quarterbacking is not acquired over night. "Men do not attain fame by sudden flight, but they, while their companions sleep, are struggling upward through the night." This is true of football quarterbacks. Correct the mistakes made in daily practice. Do not repeat them. WATCH FOR MISTAKES MADE BY OTHERS. Avoid them. Let each day find you improved in your knowledge and execution of quarterback duties.

2 important keys to leadership: Encouragement & Praise

THE QUARTERBACK MUST

a. Be the coaching staff's representative on the field.
b. Be a responsible person.
c. Be an unselfish person.
d. Be a positive thinker.
e. Be dedicated to improving every single day.
f. Have mistake-proof mechanics.

THE QUARTERBACK

- Must never show discouragement.
- Must never lose control of the huddle.
- Must never lose his poise – winners remain cool when times are toughest.
- Must never ever give up.

HUDDLE CONTROL

The QB must have total control of the huddle. You must always take charge and have the ability to keep control.

You cannot afford to be distracted; therefore, all advice or suggestions should be discussed on the sideline. The huddle should be a place of total concentration and no distractions.

You must stay away from the huddle until the play is given to you, or until you have reached a decision on what to call. Once that decision has been made, move into the huddle, call the play distinctly, never talking to fast, and never lacking authority and assurance that it is the best play. You must show poise and confidence, because without it, the play has little chance of succeeding.

Since there is often shifting, motions and other procedures that move offensive players before the snap, the speed at which the play is called in the huddle is most essential.

MECHANICS AT THE LINE OF SCRIMMAGE

You must be conscious of the habits that you develop in this area. While you're not required to be like Peyton Manning and audible 12x before the ball is snapped, you should be stereotyped from the standpoint of sweeping the defense and putting your hands under the center all at the same time. Develop the same technique to read the line defense and then scan the secondary. This is important to avoid tipping quick snap counts.

Move your team with the least possible delay, depending on the situation confronting you. You will have more of a delay when facing a defense that shifts often. Cadence is important and should stay consistent.

1 – Scan the defense.
2 – Hands under the center.
3 – Read the defense.
4 – Audible if necessary out of a bad play.
5 – If audible is called, pause to give players time to grasp new play call.

Crowd noise may cause interference with your cadence. Be aware of letting your voice falter or of speeding up or slowing down the cadence. Be positive and distinct in calling defenses and audibles…. Remember, it's not WHAT you say but HOW you say it.

RECOGNITION OF DEFENSES

Recognition of defenses is the key to play-selection and making adjustments. Why do you think you see coaches in headsets? They're trying to grasp from a bird's eye view what the defense is doing and how to adjust the best to attack the defensive strategy.

The QB must be alert and observe the key points that will give him the information he needs to run certain types of plays. For example, we may feel that the naked bootleg is a good play. It is simple to check the reactions of defensive ends and outside linebackers after the handoff. Check the reactions of the safety and linebackers after carrying out a fake. Are they respecting your position as a QB or are they just flying blindly to where they think the ball is? Knowing the defensive alignment is important.

OFFENSIVE OBJECTIVES

The function of an offense is to maintain BALL CONTROL and score as many points as possible by:

1 – Minimizing its own mistakes but magnifying the opponent's.
2 – Being able to overcome big mistakes and penalties.
3 – Having ability to gain on fundamental power plays when needed and to protect the passer.
4 – Constituting a threat in areas that opponents cannot disregard.

5 – Being able to take advantage of weaknesses as they present themselves, and keeping unrelenting pressure on the defense.
6 – Delivering the knockout blow when you have the opponent on the run. Momentum is important to have on your side.

GENERALSHIP

The Quarterback should have a good understanding of the principle of sound football strategy and tactics, a basic concept of defense, a talent for thinking through things, and a capacity for reasoning instead of grab bagging and/or reckless gambling.

In a sense, he is gambling if he does not have a purpose behind everything he does. Sound Generalship does not consist of hunches, guesses or "inspiration at the moment." It is based 90% on sound percentage football and 10% on the element of surprise.

WHAT – WHEN – WHY

Naturally, you must know WHAT you are doing, and it is important to know WHY you are doing it. But in football, it is more important to know WHEN you are supposed to do something. If you don't know the WHY and WHEN, you will fall into the class of a "grab bagger".

Leave nothing to chance. Be eager to learn the strategy of the upcoming opponent.
Repetition, or training the subconscious, until it becomes almost reflex action, is more important for a Quarterback than for any other position. The more films you study, the easier it will be for you to recognize defenses and individual tendencies. This will enable you to tactically apply the strategy successfully on game day!

QUARTERBACK FUNDAMENTALS

STANCE POSITION UNDER CENTER

a. The QB should place himself in proper position in relationship with the center for correct snap – not too far away from center and not too close. Practice snaps to find the proper position.

b. The QB should be relaxed; should be loose and not too tight or tense.

I – ARMS BENT

The arms should be bent which will help in accepting the ball from the center and will aid the QB in bringing the ball directly into the mid-section. The elbows are brought in close to the body with arms still relaxed. Having the elbows bent will aid the QB in obtaining proper distance to the center and will definitely help prevent fumbles. Arms slightly bent.

II – HEAD UP

The QB's head should be up looking straight ahead or sweeping over the field for movements by the defense or weaknesses in the defense. Head can be kept up by dropping the butt. Use same lead movement on each snap. It is important for QB to put his hands under the center while scanning the defense. If the defense is late changing, they will not align until QB puts his hands under the center. The QB can pick up many important things from alert observation of defense and defensive alignment while he is positioned behind center. This is the time to be able to call Audibles by alert observation. If the QB does not sweep the field, he is not alert and not looking over the field, he cannot call audibles or direct a team properly.

III – SHOULDERS AND BACK STRAIGHT

The QB's back should be straight and relaxed. Not too rigid. The back should not be tense. Tenseness in the back will also cause fumbles because the arms will become tense as well as the back. If the back is straight, the QB will be in proper position for quick movements and will aid in keeping the head up.

Do NOT slump or roll the shoulders over, for this will cause the head and eyes to drop down. Having the back straight will give the QB a look of alertness and is a definite psychological effect on the defense. Keep back straight and head up and look alert... be alert

IV – KNEES FLEXED

The legs of the QB should also be loose, not like poker sticks. The legs must be flexible and the QB must get his legs in terrific shape in order to have perfection in his QB play. Bending knees also gives power to begin his drop. The QB should bend his knees so that he can be in proper position to accept the ball from center and have flexibility for spinning and handing off to backs or faking. Having the knees bent is the secret to proper position and proper movements and aids in preventing fumbles. If the QB's behind center with legs straight, he almost always has to stoop over the slump or roll his shoulders to get his hands under the center. The QB must obtain the proper distance in flexibility of his knees for a relaxed and controlled stance behind center. *Relaxed.*

Bending the knees is one of the most important points. Without bend in the knees, the entire body is out of line and QB must struggle to carry out his moves.

Bent knees helps the QB to his alternate receiver. When knees are locked, pass always ends up short. Bending the knees keeps the body low, which is important for every phase and move of the QB. The bend in the knees is of the utmost importance for proper ballhandling and placement of the ball in ball carrier's stomach. Bending the knees gives the QB proper balance for all moves and aids the QB in adjusting the very situation of ball carriers.

WEIGHT ON BALLS OF FEET

The feet should be placed straight ahead and parallel to each other. Placement of the feet is important. The distance between the feet should be at a distance which will allow the QB proper balance and complete relaxation of the body. The placement of feet and bend of knees work hand in hand and should be worked together to afford the QB the position which is proper for his size and height. Obtain proper distance between feet to give necessary balance, then bend knees to obtain both balance and relaxation, then keep the back straight and keep the head and eyes up and alert.

The weight of the body is on the balls of the feet and not on the heels. This should be consistent throughout as a QB cannot spin off and move on his heels, but he can do almost anything on the balls of his feet. Heels should not be off the ground. This may cause balance problems.

Quarterback – Center Exchange

1. The top hand is sunk wrist deep. For a right handed QB, it is the right hand on top and for a lefty, the left hand goes on top.

2. Apply pressure with BOTH hands. If you push with the bottom hand, the hands should not separate when the ball is snapped into your hands.

3. Putting pressure merely insures the exchange. Don't put so much pressure that you unbalance your center. With practice, you'll find the comfort zone.

4. The fingers are spread. The thumb of the top hand is notched into the crevices of the thumb on the bottom hand. Some QB's even lock thumbs – I don't recommend this tactic.

5. The QB keeps his hands as close together as possible as the center snaps the ball. As the football hits the pressure hand, the trap or bottom hand closes on the ball. Keep the heels of the hands together. (See QB Center Exchange Photo)

6. When the QB receives the ball, the QB rides the center forward with his arms to ensure a good clean exchange. The elbows must extend inward on the snap, and this allows the QB to begin to fall back and begin his drop.

7. After the QB receives the ball from center, he immediately brings the ball to the stomach to the bottom of the numbers parallel to the ground. The QB should keep both hands on the ball. This technique is called "seating the ball."

8. A critical error occurs when the QB relaxes his hand pressure somewhere between the time the snap count is called and when the ball actually arrives. The center must feel pressure all the way until the ball actually hits the QB's hands.

9. A second critical error occurs when the QB relaxes his under hand and looses control of the snap or gets his fingers jammed.

** If you or your QB are having problems fumbling the QB/Center Exchange, go over each of these data points and assess the problem. You should NEVER have a fumble in a game from a QB/Center exchange gone bad!

QB PIVOTS

PIVOT

1. The pivot is always made with the ball of the foot with either the right or left foot depending on the pivot and which direction the QB is moving.

2. The heel must be elevated.

3. All pivots are started by taking the weight on the foot opposite the pivot foot.

4. Then the QB pushes hard off the push foot and then the QB will rotate about the ball of the pivot foot which now has assumed the weight of the body.

5. Turn head and shoulders first! The head must always precede the pivot.

6. EXTREMELY IMPORTANT – Twist or turn pivot foot and step off on the other foot in direction of the handoff. Get ball as deep as possible to the ball carrier and with quickness. (Each running play is different and requires proper footwork for the timing of the play – work with your coach for each specific run play.

7. Avoid false stepping!

8. The greatest problem on pivoting is a raising up and down of the shoulders during the

pivot action. QB's should be comfortable and consistent in this motion.

9. Common error is that the QB does not keep his knees bent throughout the pivot cycle.

10. Prior to practicing the footwork that is required in the run or the pass, the QB is given a frame of reference upon which to execute his initial movements away from the center. The QB can now be instructed to pivot to any hour of the clock between three and nine to establish the correct movement path away from the center. The toes of the QB must end the pivot and face in the direction that is required.

11. DO NOT FALSE STEP!

** Pivoting is required on every running play. Whether it is a 24/25 counter, a 22/23 lead, a 31/32 quick trap, whatever the play is called – it is CRITICAL that a QB does NOT false step. A false step will lead to collisions with the running back, lost fumbles, poor running back/ quarterback exchanges and loss of yardage against strong defenses.

QB HANDOFFS

Handoffs

1. The handoff is the responsibility of the QB. Don't gamble if you can't make a proper handoff. Follow the back into the hole or eat the ball.

2. The QB should work with the football from his stomach area. Keep the ball seated and tucked – with both hands on the ball – until the handoff is made.

3. The QB should move with quick, short steps. The QB should pick up the ball and focus in on the target area where the ball will be placed. This is the QB's 1st responsibility.

4. The eyes are the most important phase of the QB's mechanics. A QB must learn to turn his head with his eyes locating the spot where the ball should be placed. The QB must watch the handoff spot until the ball is placed against it. "Look the ball in." The ball should be still as it is placed in the ball carrier's stomach. Do not SLAM or THROW the ball into the ball carriers stomach. The arm should be bent to allow an extension adjustment to the RB's path if necessary.

5. The QB will come to a brief pause or stop as he hands the ball off. The QB will let his

hand "ride" with the ball carrier. This pause or "ride" comes at the end of the exchange.

6. Placement of the football should be with a light hand – do not jam or push the ball in the ball carrier's stomach. Often QBs will place the ball on the target spot but let it slide from it before the ball carrier folds over it. Make sure you're consistent in your exchange.

7. The QB should work from navel to navel.

8. The QB will remove the closest hand before the ball is placed into the running back. The ball is given to the running back with the palm up.

9. The motion is always slightly from low to high and never vice-versa. The QB should work the football up into the running back's pcket. The QB should "flow" with the running back and let the back's momentum force his hand off the ball.

10. After the handoff, the QB should fake to keep the ball with proper footwork, but make sure of the handoff first. Don't be in a hurry. Stay low and keep the shoulders down so you don't give easy tips to the defense.

11. When the QB coach can not watch the exchange, the coach should continually ask the QB between repetitions, "how was the handoff?" and "where was the ball placed?"

– these questions force the QB to focus everytime.

12. Use the same handoff techniques with play action passes.

QB FAKING

Faking

1. The play action pass is probably the best single way to throw the football. The play action pass occurs when the QB fakes a run play prior to throwing the ball.

2. It is stronger to fake the run play to the side of the QB's throwing arm. If the QB can open up and fake to his front side, he can take a normal drop with more speed.

3. The key to play passing is not the QB fake, but the man he's faking to. The QB can fool a lot of people but the back is the man the linebackers and secondary are looking at – especially at the lower levels of football. As soon as that back's shoulders come up, the LB knows that he doesn't have the ball. A big part of play action passing is the fake man's shoulder being waist high.

4. When the QB fakes, he should extend the ball briefly in front of the man and before he gets there, take the ball away and leave your hand in and let the back go by. Your job as the QB is to "SELL" the play fake. Watch Peyton Manning do this, it is like magic!

5. Key: extend the ball early and operate at the hip level. The ball is shown between the running back and the linebacker.

34

6. The QB should extend the ball, letting the man ride and then put the ball in the stomach region.

7. The key is, How much does it look like the actual running play? The QB and RB will determine the success of a play action pass more than anyone else.

8. STEPS: what step do you hand it off of? The same steps should be taken on play action passes.

Coaching Point

Anytime you can deceive the defense or use a defense's aggression against itself is advantageous to the offense. A strong QB fake can make a QB completion percentage increase by 20-30% just because it puts the defense that much further out of position. Work hard on play action fakes and making sure they are "sold" and not just going through the motions.

CADENCE

Cadence

1. The cadence is THE MOST IMPORTANT advantage an offense has. Nothing can frustrate a defense more than when it jumps offsides in critical situations. The QB controls the rhythm and timing of the cadence.

Here are a few examples of a cadence:

"Go" – "Black 20" "Black 20" – "Sethut!"

The advantage of that cadence is that you can go on "1st sound" or you can use a color to make an audible change. For example, if the audible color is YELLOW, a QB could use the follow cadence:

"Go" – "Black 11" – "Check Check" – "Yellow 23" "Yellow 23" – "Sethut"

If you are a little league team and you want a simple cadence, something like this usually works great:

"Down" (Pause 1 or 2 seconds) "Set" (Again Pause) "Hike!" (Snap the ball)

If you were to go "on 2" in this example it would sound like this:

"Down" – Pause – "Set" – Pause – "Hike!" –Pause – "Hike!" (Snap the ball)

2. Another point to consider here is if you are using audibles in your system then make sure the QB uses numbers in his dummy call that are familiar and common to your offensive system so that when you are audibling the defense will not now because you have been using the same numbers in your dummy audibles.

** Coaching Point **

Keep the cadence consistent. Make sure each player understands what the exact time of the snap will be. Also, be quick but be patient. Pacing in your calls is important and will help your offense develop a rhythm. A strong quarterback uses the cadence in his teams favor.

Movement Away From Center

1. SPEED

A – Speed is the 1st thing that comes to mind and the only way to obtain speed is to practice and think speed. Speed and quickness is one of the 1st steps in obtaining the play's goal.

2. MOVEMENT

The movement away from the center call for different parts of the body to move in unison.

- Movement of the feet
- Movement of the knees (flexed)
- Movement of the hips
- Movement of the shoulders
- Movement of the head
- Head up

All movements are in unison. The QB should be able to move without calling attention to any one thing. All these separate movements should be combined into one smooth and fluid motion – all with great speed.

When the QB spins, he should be on balance and have one of his feet in direction he is moving. If the QB spins on his right foot, he should point his left foot in the direction he is moving to the ball carrier. The plancement of the foot will vary with the play and hole as well as the direcetion and amount of spin of the QB. So, when a QB thinks "movement" – he should think of speed, quickness, placement of the feet, elbows bent, stay low and head up with body on balance.

3. SETTING TO PASS

Once QB gets the ball from center, the QB leans to help carry himself back to the set up point. The QB will pivot on his push-off foot with great speed. The QB must master retreating from the center. For the right-handed QB, the push off foot is his left foot. QB must put pressure on the ball of the foot. The QB on a 5-step drop will take 3 big steps and 2 small gather steps. The QB must transfer his weight to the push foot, always keeping his head and eyes turned up field, not to his rear as he steps backward.

The success in passing is very dependent upon how long it takes for the QB to get back and be in position to pass. After the pivot, the QB points his feet on a 45-degree angle and retreats with great speed but under complete control.

As the QB retreats, he must be conscious of quickness but steps must be predicated on balance. Big steps with proper weight balance are critical to co-ordinated throws. Stepping and setting to throw stop must be precise. The QB can NOT take extra steps to gain balance. The QB must learn how to lower hs center of gravity by sinking his hips, by bending his knees.

The 1st step away from the center is the most important. Get depth. Push away from the center and gain depth. Get separation from the line of scrimmage equally on 3 and 5 step drops.

As the QB retreats, he will gather himself and be able to set up at either 3 steps, 5 steps from the line of scrimmage; <u>as the QB retreats, his head should be looking straight up field.</u> This eye skill prevents the defense from knowing where the ball is going to be thrown or to what receiver. When the QB gets to his last step, he is in position to throw to any direction and has his body in proper placement so he can step into the direction of the receiver – always stepping and pointing the front foot at the receiver.

Also – the front elbow is close to the body and the front shoulder is down as you retreat so that the weight will not be on the wrong foot when the QB sets up.

The last 2 steps are gather steps and not hop steps. The QB should not hop back on his last step and throw his weight on his right foot and hip. The QB should have the weight fall on the last step or front foot – gathering his feet and legs so they are in good position for a move in any direction and his front shoulder must be lower that throwing shoulder.

The QB should hesitate after gathering into his last step so that he can be in position and on balance to throw a perfect pass to the reciver. Every pass is different and every receiver is different so the QB should work until he is well acquainted with every pattern of pass and every receiver.

TIMING is one of the most important phases of passing. Know your receivers, work with them until your footwork and your drop is perfectly timed with the movements of all receivers.

** Coaching Point **

If a wide receiver is running a route that is either too short or too long for the QB's movements, it will wreak havoc on the QB's ability to Set Up to Pass. Make sure that the route combinations fit the movement of the QB and vice versa. Otherwise, it will be interception city!

QB PASS DROPS

Getting to the passing drop

- There is a spot from which each pass should be thrown and there is a preferred type of footwork to use in reaching each spot. It is critical that your offensive lineman and blockers know where that spot is so they can give you the best possible protection.

- It is also vital that this passing spot be coordinated with the break of the receivers so that the QB is "SET" and "READY" to throw BEFORE the receiver makes his break. Learn these passing spots and how to get to them. Work to improve quickness in getting to the preferred passing spot with good depth. Rhythm and Timing are EVERYTHING when it comes to passing.

3 Step Drop

a. The 3 step drop is a "punch" step and 1-2-3 plant on the 3rd step and throw. The QB will either take 3 quick steps and throw or he will take 3 big steps and throw. The size of the steps will be determined by the receivers route.

b. The "punch" or "separation" step allows the Q to get a little further back before he starts his actual drop. He must keep his eyes ahead to freeze the coverage momentarily.

c. The QB must REACH hard on his 1st step. Separation from the center on the 1st step is crucial. Open the hips and keep the body weight forward over the left foot. The QB must also keep his left shoulder downfield or slightly open. The QB will pivot on his left foot. Get good body lean for momentum.

d. The 2nd step is a crossover step that allows the QB to gain depth. It's important not to step over the midline.

e. The 3rd step is a stretch step; once more gaining depth. It is on this step that the QB comes out throwing the ball. He must maintain his body weight over his front foot.

f. The QB must be prepared to pivot and throw as the 3rd step hits the ground.

Reach back slightly and kick the heel out when throwing left.

g. Look straight upfield as the QB goes back seeing the keys and defensive men as QB goes.

h. Timed throw – 1,2,3 – front shoulder open body lean: hips over shoulders.

i. Open (1) – Crossover (2) – Hit (3) and throw. Keep shoulder down. Depth not critical issue – rhythm and timing are much more important on quick drops.

Coaching Point

On 3 step drops, the most important key is quickness. Get back away from the center quickly and have your feet in proper position to throw the ball. If you are not "on time" with a 3 step drop, you are setting yourself up for disaster. Big – little – little – THROW!

5 Step Drop

1 – Once the QB has taken the snap, pull the ball to the stomach region and then up to the chest region in one smooth motion.

2 – We start with a 4-6 inch "Punch" step with the left foot (right handers). This helps get the QB a little further back before he starts his drop. On the snap count, the QB drops his left foot and it hits the ground just when the ball hits the QB's hands. This get the forward leaning pre-snap QB going backwards with some momentum. This step is not counted.

3 – The 1st step is a "reach" step. The QB must pivot on the left foot and then reach step toward the passing spot with the right. Pivot on the left foot and then reach step toward the passing spot with the right foot. This is the 1st step the QB takes. This is almost where the QB sits down somewhat. He must keep his weight low by keeping his buttocks low. QB pulls his right elbow and right hip around. On this step, the QB must open up and get depth and separation from the center. He must open down the midpoint and not beyond. A bad first step closes the hips. This step also builds body lean and momentum.

4 – The next step is a "crossover step" with the left foot. QB must drive and crossover. 2nd step is a crossover for body lean and momentum.

5 – The QB must open his shoulders – a 45 degree angle to the line of scrimmage – and look

straight upfield, seeing his keys and defensive men as the QB retreats. Know whether the primary receiver will be open by the time you reach the passing spot.

6 – Step 3 is a depth step. A step of control. Also called a "stretch step" – the first 3 steps are the key to get the QB away from the pass rush. During these steps the QB must be conscious of keeping the ball up and keeping the front elbow close to the body and the front shoulder is down.

7 – Bent knees help the QB to adjust, step and throw. This is vital for the QB to hit his alternate receiver. When the knees are locked, the pass always ends up short.

8 – Step 4 with the left foot is not a hop step. This is a smaller step. This step will help the QB to regain balance and to slow momentum away from line of scrimmage.

9 – Step 5 is the final step and is referred to as the break foot. Once again, this is a small step. This will ensure that the QB will stop in the "ready" position and be ready to throw. The QB should have the weight fall on the last step or front foot – gathering his feet and lesgs so that the QB is in a position for a move in any direction. On 5th step, the QB should be under control and balanced up.

10 – After reaching the required depth (5 step drop = 7 yards deep) – the QB will plant the right foot and then step forward on the left as the throwing motion starts. The QB must now shift his weight when throwing to give passes more speed

and power. The QB must step in the direction of the receiver for a strong accurate throw.

11 – Keep your feet under you at the setup point. This is your throwing platform. Step directly at the target. Check for "overstriding" or "stepping off" if the ball sails or goes into the dirt.

12 – Make sure weight is transferred to front foot. This is one of the most important points. Back leg should come off the ground and there should be a bend in the front leg.

13 – The QB wants to keep his toes, torso, and eyes pointed to the receiver.

14 – During the drop, the QB must try to keep his forehead parallel to the line of scrimmage.

15 – As the QB drops back, ask him to look straight up the field. If he can find the left one third up field, he will be able to find the right side up field.

16 – Consistency is most important. Find a flow and rhythm and practice it 1,000 times!

17 – Let feet take the QB through the progression.

18 – Never close the shoulder opposite the throwing side.

19 – Lead with the belt buckle. This technique helps the QB to open his hips and step in

the direction he wants to throw. "Lead with the belt buckle."

20 – Releasing the ball above the shoulder helps create a natural follow through motion.

21 – Feet. With the QB position, the placement of the feet are more important than any other position on the team.

COACHING TIP

Understand that all QB's are going to have different movements. The key is to have speed and timing, and that a QB is always on balance in the drop.
BIG – BIG – BIG – LITTLE – LITTLE – THROW!

QB PASS DROPS from the SHOTGUN FORMATION

SHOTGUN

- The QB will align in a stance directly behind the center with his heels set at 5 yards deep.

- The QB will continue to set up on his 3-5-7 step drops at the same depth as always.

- The Shot Gun will improve the vision of the QB as far as seeing the defense. The separation the QB has from the rush gives the QB a better picture of the play developing.

- As soon as the ball reaches the QB's hands, he begins his pass drops and scans the defense as his receivers run their routes.

- The QB uses the same motion to reach his pass drop as he does in his normal drop-back technique.

** COACHING TIP**

The shotgun formation forces plays to "take longer" because the time from the center snap to the time the QB receives the football is longer than a direct snap from under center. A QB needs to understand that his depth allows him to get to his passing

release point sooner. Don't be in a hurry to throw
the ball when you're in the shotgun formation.
Allow the flow of the play to mature – and don't
take any sacks in the shotgun!

QB GRIP

GRIP

    a. The QB places his fingers on the laces.

    b. The QB places his little finger just below the 4th lace. He places his middle finger at the top of the laces resting.

    c. The index and middle finger are the last to leave the ball. These two fingers are the ones that impact the spin on the ball.

    d. The thumb is placed underneath the ball and should be 3" from the pint. Perpendicular to the panels on the ball.

    e. After gripping the ball, adjust your hand slightly until it feels comfortable.

** COACHING POINT **

Every QB will have a different "grip" on the ball. The key is to practice and make it consistent. When a QB has hit expert level, he will be able to adjust and throw the ball quickly without laces. The grip is the "sweet spot" for the QB and should be consistent.

PASSING THE FOOTBALL

QB PASSING

a. Individual physical differences can
    necessitate different styles for passing
    the ball. Each technique will be
    appropriate for the individual involved.

b. The FEET initiate the entire movement.
    A small step forward transfers the body
    weight from the back foot to the front
    foot, thus giving the body momentum as
    the ball is thrown. Hip Rotation should
    occur during the stride.

c. It is a common mistake to throw off the
    back foot. This will cause you to throw
    inaccurate passes with no velocity.
    Remember – the back foot is the plant
    foot, like a pitcher on a pitcher's mound,
    and should be used to brake and push off
    of toward your target.

d. The lead step must be slight off set of
    the target. This allows complete hip
    rotation. Check lead step for loss of
    velocity also.

e. The back leg should be slightly flexed
    before initiation of the lead step. This
    allows full body momentum to transfer
    into the throw. Some QBs block their hip
    rotation by not opening up that lead foot
    enough. Throwing across the body

results in a floating, wobbly pass.
QUACK QUACK!

f. As the weight comes forward the hips
    rotate and in effect uncoil the torso
    thereby providing additional momentum.
    This rotation is counterclockwise.

g. The release itself is accomplished by
    forearm pronation and wrist flexion.
    Pronation is an outward rotation of the
    forearm which results in the hand
    finishing with palm facing the ground
    and thumb directly at the ground.

h. The snap of the wrist is important
    because it adds velocity and spiral action
    as the fingers leave the ball in sequence
    from the little finger to the index finger.

i. It is the index finger and wrist snap
    impart the number of spirals on the ball.

j. Additional importance in the delivery is
    the fact that the elbow should lead the
    throwing motion. This ensures that the
    nose of the ball is up and results in a
    softer easier pass to catch. Elbow should
    always be as high or higher than the
    shoulder.

k. The football should be held comfortably
    at the upper chest level. Do NOT drop
    the ball or be lazy with the ball low. It
    slows down your delivery.

1. The back leg should leave the ground on completion of the throwing motion.

** COACHING TIP **

If there is frustration from lack of consistency in throwing spirals and/or hitting the target, the QB needs to practice with repetition more. Make sure that you are not asking the QB to do more than his arm strength and/or mental make up allows. A QB who sees failure over and over has a difficult time being a team leader and oozing the confidence he needs to lead his team. Practice the drop and the repetition at least 1,000 times!

FOOTWORK IN PASSING

QB Footwork in Passing

a. The QB will be in the best position to
    throw if he is in the "ready" position and
    has proper balance. He should be able to
    move laterally or forward to get in the
    best passing lane. Then use the proper
    footwork to pass the ball.

    - ONE STEP – the basic throwing
      footwork from the "ready" position
      is a short step with the forward foot,
      parallel to the target line, push off
      the rear foot and throw. Bring the
      rear foot up off the ground balancing
      on the forward foot.

    - SHUFFLE – When the QB needs
      more power and in some cases for
      accuracy, shuffle along the target
      line then use the one-step technique
      and throw.

    - STATIONARY – When unable to
      one-step or shuffle because of a rush,
      push weight to the forward foot and
      throw.

COMMON PASSING ERRORS

1 – Poor timing.
- Throw the ball as the receiver is coming into the clear: do not wait until he is already there. The release time is dictated by the movement of the arrival of the receiver.

2 – Underthrown Pass
- Underthrown passes result from poor follow through or overstriding. If a ball is released late from overhand throw, it will be short of the target. A pass will fall short if the step with the left foot is taken too soon or if the step is too large.
- Also, if the arm is not fully extended, if it is cramped down near the head, the ball will be underthrown.

3 – Loss of Lateral Accuracy
- If the QB is throwing in front or behind the receiver the passing motion is no longer overhand but sidearm. A side arm passer is less accurate horizontally while and overhand passer is apt to be more inaccurate vertically. A sidearm throw can be spotted

by watching the end of the
follow through.

4 – Loss of Spiral
- In most instances loss of
spiral is due to the wrist
being twisted at the moment
of release instead of being
snapped forward. If the wrist
doesn't snap forward, the ball
flutters. Lock the wrist at all
times.

5 – Throwing Across the Body
- When you do not step
directly at your intended
target, you are not
mechanically sound in your
motion and release.
Throwing across the body is
due to the QB not stepping
directly at the intended
receiver. Throwing across
the body diminishes power
and accuracy.

6 – Concentrating on the Intended Receiver
- From the time the ball is
snapped until the time it is
thrown, the QB should NOT
stare down or constantly look
at the intended receiver.
Good defensive players are
taught to "read the
quarterbacks eyes" and if the
QB is staring down just one

receiver, the defense will have lots of interceptions because they are anticipating the throw!

7 – Poor Ball Control

- When the QB drops back the ball should be held chest high. When the rear foot is planted and set to throw the ball the QB does not want to have to bring the ball back up. This is wasted motion – and it's also slow motion. A good QB must be mechanically sound.

8 – False Step

- After the snap of the ball the QB jab steps up and pushes off that foot and retreats. Valuable seconds are lost due to this faulty footwork. False steps are typical reasons for late throws. Do NOT false step!

9 – Overstriding

- When you overstride, you elongate the throwing motion and that results in a late release which then forces the tip of the ball downward. The ball typically ends up short of the target.

10 – Understriding

- Shortened throwing motion with the ball being released too early, resulting in the tip being elevated. The ball simply "sails" or takes off and the famous "balloon" ball occurs. Balloon balls get popped!

6 STEP SEQUENCE TO THROWING THE FOOTBALL

Follow these simple 6 steps to throw a good football pass – over and over again.

1 – Grip the ball properly.

2 – Push the ball into the throwing motion.

3 – The weight is then totally on the right side, resting on the rear, or right leg which is firmly planted. Left arm is pulled down and away as shoulders rotate.

4 – Weight transfer, which provides the power for the throw, begins with the left leg lifted slightly and the left arm moving toward the target. This will open up the left hip, so important for accuracy, because the QB must face the player to whom he is throwing.

5 – As the ball is cocked and ready to throw, the right elbow will lead the way as the forward arm motion begins with the right wrist firmly locked.

6 – The weight transfer will be completed with the left foot on the ground as the right wrist and forearm catch up with the hips and the ball is released just past the head. Stay on the ball of the left foot on stride, heel first is the problem.

THE PERFECT "FORM"

Perfect Form

1 – Short lead step with left foot. Think "CHIN OVER TOES."

2 – Receiver framed between feet. Think "BELT BUCKLE POINTED TO TARGET."

3 – High Release. Think "ELBOW HIGH – BALL WILL FLY!"

4 – Palm and thumb down on release. Think "PALM DOWN for TOUCHDOWN".

** COACHING TIPS **

As you've continued to read this book, you've learned that repetition, repetition, repetition is the key to success. If a QB just threw a "balloon ball" over the head of his receiver and you want to coach him up fast, just simply say "Chin over toes." – These cues sink in quickly and will help the quarterback compartmentalize each aspect of his throwing motion.

QB PASSING LANES

PASSING LANES

Have you ever seen Drew Brees or Tom Brady side step or move forward in the pocket after they've hit their position to throw the ball? They're not panicking, they're simply moving in the pocket to find the passing lanes. Without a passing lane, your pass will likely be knocked down by a defender.

Passing Lanes – The most important thing the QB must do after he sets up is to find the throwing lane. This means the QB can move in an area of about one square yard, left and right. When he comes back and sets up he can move left or right to find the opening. If the passes are getting batted down, the QB is not throwing the ball over through the passing lane.

If the QB has to throw the ball over people, he tends to throw it high. We will use the "Wave Drill" to simulate what happens to a QB during the game. On the drill the QB does not want to move a great deal. He moves his feet just enough to make the defensive lineman miss him. As the QB moves, the ball should not move below his breast. The QB is not scrambling: he is moving within the pocket. He is finding the throwing lane.

Remember, there is a huge difference between finding a passing lane and scrambling. When you scramble, you are literally "on your own" because the offensive lineman have their back to you. They can not see where you are, so they expect you to stay in the pocket – if you scramble out, you do so at your own risk and you are likely to take strong defensive hits outside the pocket.

Find your passing lane. Deliver the ball on time. Distribute the ball to your playmakers. If you can do that – you'll be on your way to QB stardom!

COMMON QB MISTAKES TO BE ALERT FOR

COMMON QB MISTAKES

1 – Pressure to center on the QB/center exchange. Must keep hands in proper position with firm pressure that center can feel.

2 – Keep weight on the balls of feet, not heels, this will help QB from pulling away too soon.

3 – Left foot or drive foot of right handed passer can be slightly staggered to help eliminate false steps. We DO NOT LIKE FALSE STEPS!

4 – Must take pre-snap read of the defense, both front and secondary. Believe with proper preparation QB can read coverage before the snap most of the time. Great advantage for QB to know the percentage receiver and proper check off receiver before the snap.

5 – Reinforcement key as QB drops to throwing spot. Use different keys for various patterns, safety is most often used… where is the safety lined up before the snap? Is the middle of the field open or closed?

6 – Must stomach the ball immediately after the exchange. Move ball to comfortable position about numbers high on drop back pass.

7 – Many young QBs have bad habits and they carry the ball too high or too low, which results in a long wind up when releasing the football.

8 – Set position of feet is very important: a strong QB must have bend in back knee or drive leg. Must also get back toes or ball of back foot turned in proper direction of throw.

9 – Keep feet working. Do not wait for a WR to be open because we throw the ball on time. If he is waiting, throw to a different receiver.

10 – Drive off back leg, good follow thru, do not overstride.

11 – Must practice all types of drop. Be able to use correct drop with each type of route and check down.

12 – QB and receivers must know what to do when flushed out of the pocket. Have the receiver on side of slush turn upfield and all the rest work laterally in direction of the QB.

CAUSES OF INTERCEPTIONS

Why do interceptions happen?

1. Don't throw off balance.

- Off balance passing is often caused by poor protection, by the QB leaving pocket or by simply throwing late, allowing the rushers to force the ball into the air. Of one thing you can be sure; If your body is not moving toward the target as the ball is thrown, then you must counteract the loss of body motion by increasing the ball's trajectory. Increased trajectory means more time for the defense to cover and the answer is an obvious one.

2. Don't throw behind the receiver.

- Assuming the receiver has whipped the defender, to throw behind the receiver is in effect to throw the ball TO the defender. Better to overthrow than to under throw.

3. Don't throw over linebacker: throw between linebackers.

- To throw over a linebacker it softens a pass so that a deep back can intercept it. Very often an experienced passer can help the receiver get open on a short pass by making a quick fake to pull the linebacker off the receiver.

4. Don't throw late

- Inexperienced passers are prone to do this. Very often this type of passer waits until the receiver is wide open before he throws the ball. By the time the ball gest there the cover has taken effect and the receiver is covered. What the passer must do is to throw the ball the instant the receiver begins to get open, and then by the time the ball gets there the receiver is wide open.

5. Don't throw a long pass short.

- Since the purpose of a long pass is to throw over the deep defender any long pass thrown short of this will in effect be

thrown to the deep
defender. On the other
hand, if you overthrow
the long pass it can only
result in an incompletion
while the under thrown
long pass most certainly
will result in an
interception.

6. Don't throw a short pass long.

- Short passes should be
  aimed no higher than the
  shoulders, for a ball
  thrown at finger-tip
  height on a short pass will
  often result in what we
  call a volleyball
  interception, one that has
  been touched but not
  caught. You must
  remember that anytime a
  ball is not caught and
  remains in the air, the
  defense has a much better
  chance of caching it that
  the offense because the
  defenders are converging
  on the ball while there is
  usually only one receiver
  in the vicinity. The ball
  that has been tipped and
  not caught has lost its
  speed and it flutters down
  like an autumn leaf into

the awaiting hands of a defender. From these two coaching points we have derived the coaching admonition. "Never throw a long pass short and never throw a short pass long." It is best to keep short passes low and away from the defender.

7. Don't allow receivers to become bunched.

- When they do they merely bring extra defenders into the area. As the QB sees this situation arise, do not pass the ball – you simply can not force the ball through a crowd. Never force a pass.

8. Don't allow receivers to run curves, but allow angles instead.

- Running an angle course that at some place on that course the receiver will come open, but on a curved course he can be covered all the way. Receivers should be sharp and crisp coming in and

out of their breaks – NO
BANANA ROUTES.

9. Don't use desperate heaves

- Don't use this to get your
  team out of trouble for it
  will merely get into more
  trouble.

10. Don't throw deep passes on obvious
passing downs.

- For the defense will be
  back waiting for that ball.
  There is one exception to
  this coaching point. If
  you find that the defense
  is playing tight on third
  down to cut off the out of
  trouble pass, then it is a
  calculated risk to throw
  deep, for you are NOW
  wagering an interception
  against a touchdown.

** COACHING TIPS **

The past 10 directions have all talked about "what not to do" – and the fact is that you can do some of those things and get away with it. The key is to take calculated risks. For example, if it's 3rd and 12 on your own 38 yard line with 20 seconds left in the half, it's not a big deal to throw a deep pass that gets intercepted. More than likely your team would punt the next down anyway, so an interception – assuming the defender is tackled instantly – could actually benefit you and your team.

The bottom line is that as QB, you have to be SUPER SMART. You have to know down and distance. You have to know blitz situations. You have to know who your "hot receiver" is if a certain defender blitzes. Take smart risks – and go win the game!

QUARTERBACK DRILLS

Foot quickness drills

1. **Shifting the feet**

    a. **Execution** – QB executes the 5 step drop technique. Must remember all techniques pertaining to drop. On 5th step set, QB coach gives hand signals right – left – center and then the QB set himself in direction of signal. Then coach gives the command "throw" and QB throws to player the coach has signaled to.

    b. **Purpose** – to make the QB move his feet and set up quickly. Weight on balls of feet, keep feet under you and step to lead and throw – passing action.

2. **Shuffle Drill – Wave and Scramble**

    a. **Execution** – QB sets to pass on 5 steps, then is directed by a wave of the hand to move either to the left or back to the right and then forward and then back. When the coach wants the ball thrown, he raises his hand and the QB throws at that moment.

b. **Purpose** – help the QB's movement within the pocket – quick feet!

3. **Bag Drills**

   a. **Facing Forward** – good football position, ball tucked away, forward and back. Emphasis – body and weight control. We use the same drill going back to our starting position.

   b. **Step Over** – Facing forward, lead step over dummy both feet in each hole, never crossing over. It is near foot over the dummies. Emphasis – foot speed and body control. Never cross over. We use the same drill going back to our starting position.

   c. **Shuffle Drill** – Facing the dummies, eyes down field in passing stance, shuffle forward and back not looking at the ground, even if a bag has been moved. Never crossing over. Emphasis – must learn to feel what is happening at your feet. Body and foot control maintaining proper throwing position. We us the same drill going back. The players back will be to the bags. After the players go through the bags, they are to spring 10 yards to a cone. They make one move at the cone and move through. We have a manager at the cone. If the manager slaps the player it means to go again, because he did not make a good move at the cone. They must keep two hands on the ball at all times in the 3 drills. If I can knock the ball out of their hands they have to do 10 pushups. I want them to keep their eyes downfield.

LOOSENING UP THE ARM

a. **Knee Drill**

- Execution – Place the knee of the throwing hand on the ground and thrown from this position. QB's are 10 yards apart.

- Purpose – Get QB to open up torso to target – swing elbow to get hips and shoulders around – keep feet still – shoulders square to target.

b. **Squaring the Shoulder**

- Execution – 2 QBs – 10 yards apart. QB raises up on toes

and goes through mechanics of throwing the football.

- Purpose – To help QB throw in a straight downward motion also helps QB to gain some added height when throwing the ball.

c. **Front Foot Drill**

- Execution – QB face each other 10 yards apart. QB raises up on toes and goes through mechanics of throwing the ball.

- Purpose – To help QB throw in a straight downward motion and also helps QB to gain some added height when throwing the ball.

d. **Throwing on the Run**

- Execution – 2 QBs run along parallel lines 10 yards apart. Concentrate on throwing the ball with the shoulders open to the target. Pull elbow back to square up shoulder. Maintain high arm action – smooth release – keep feet under you.

- Purpose – Sharpen skill of throwing directly at receiver and not leading him.

e. Circle Drill

- Execution – QB jogs around the coach. Throws to the coach 5 times clockwise and 5 throws counterclockwise. Get shoulders square around – keep feet under and pull elbow back to help square up shoulder.

- Purpose – Proper techniques when throwing a sprint out pass.

f. Touch Drill

- Execution – QB starts on a line 10 yards in front of the goalposts and when QB reaches center support post turns his shoulders and passes ball over crossbar. Successful only if the ball skims over the bar and into the arms of someone standing behind the goalposts. Can be repeated from opposite direction to perfect action from either side.

- Purpose – Improves QBs ability to drop the ball between linebackers and defensive backs on the move.

DROPBACK DRILL TECHNIQUES

DROP BREAK DOWN DRILLS

1 – Punch and Reach

- Sit down as you step back with the left foot on the snap, then reach back with the right foot as you pivot on the left.

2 – Punch and Reach – Cross Over

- Crossover with your left foot right down the mid-line.

3 – Punch – Reach – Cross Over – Stretch

- Stretch long on your right step.

4 – Punch – Reach – Crossover – Stretch – Set 'Em

- Begin to gather your momentum as you prepare to stop.

5 – Punch – Reach – Crossover – Stretch – Set 'Em – Hitch

- Stop by digging on the insides of your right foot, and then push off and slide step forward in the pocket one step.

BAG DRILL

1 – **Execution** – QB takes a 5 step drop. Receiver hesitates tehn puts his hands up as if just coming open. The coach simulates pressure in the pocket by hitting the QB with the bag just as the QB releases the ball.

2 – **Purpose** – Stress concentration downfield, follow through with weight transfer to front left coach makes contact in chest area on side opposite throwing arm coach works both sides from passing side allow follow thru and contact on back shoulder.

3 –5 STEP DROP DRILL

1 – **Execution** – QBs drop along a yard stripe to check each proper drop.

2 – **Purpose** – In any drop check speed to drop point. First 3 steps are important to get separation. Two hands on the ball carried across chest region. Keep feet under (throwing platform). Step directly at target (check for overstriding) Check hips and shoulders. Check transfer of weight to front foot. Back leg off the ground. Check depth and timing of drop.

QUICK RELEASE DRILL – RECOGNITION DRILL

1 – Execution – Have QB dropback – 3 or 5 steps – and have 2 or 3 receivers positioned in designated areas. When the QB hits his last step of the drop, one of the receivers flash his hands off the ball. The QB then steps up and throws as quickly as he can while working on accuracy.

2 – Purpose – Helps QB develop a quick release plus working on the basic drop techniques. Use a play so QB can work on progression footwork. Keep feet moving while going through progression.

AVOID THE RUSH DRILL

The QB drops to set up depth. If you are a 5-step drop passing team use that. If you are a 7-step drop, team use that. If you are a shotgun team, use that. The coach stands facing the QB. The QB takes the snap and drops to 7.5 yars, sets his feet and THEN the coach gives the QB a direction with his arm. This is to assimilate the QB avoiding the rush, 2 or 3 yards to the one side or the other, and then the QB resets and throws to a stationary target 10-15 yards down field. The important part is not the throw, it is how fst the QB moves east or west and rests their feet. This drill allows your QB to become a passer rather than a scrambler. This teaches the QB to keep his shoulders perpendicular with the line of scrimmage and in a position to pass the ball. Once your QB turns his shoulders he is in a scrambling mode. He is out of the passing position. We want to keep the QB in passing position throughout this drill.

Top 10 Attributes of a Dominant QB

a. Decision Making
b. Accuracy
c. Toughness
d. Footwork
e. Leadership
f. Arm Strength
g. Cool, Calm, Collected
h. Mistake Free
i. Coach's Trust
j. Are you having fun?

TOP 10 ATTRIBUTES of a DOMINANT QB

1 – Decision Making.

Close your eyes and think of the best QB's that you can think of – names like Tom Brady, Drew Brees, Peyton Manning, Steve Young, Joe Montana and many others probably come to mind.

While it's obvious that each of those quarterbacks have amazing physical skills that have been honed and polished through years and years of practice, but it's even more obvious that they have the most important factor in being a dominant quarterback – each of them are fantastic decision-makers.

Situation: It's 1st and 10 on my team's 23 yard line and coach calls a play action pass, there is a strong weakside linebacker rush and my options are limited, I can:

A: Throw the ball away
B: Try to run away from the pressure and make a play with my feet
C: Take the sack
D: Force a hurried pass into a covered receiver

Which one would you choose?

While the answer may seem obvious at 1st glance, it unleashes a furry of other questions about the situation. What quarter is it? Are we in the lead or are we behind? What is the score? Who has the momentum right now? What are the chances if I throw this hurried pass into a covered receiver that it will be caught? How confident am I that I can get this pass in there? How confident am I that if I do throw it that my teammate will be ready to catch this?

Each one of those questions is valid. And the outcome of that one single play can be a turning point in the game…. either good or bad. The problem is the decision that you make, either A, B, C, or D – all have to be made within 3 seconds or less! Talk about pressure!

That is why QB's are students of the game and understand situational football. They have to live with the risks they do take – but also the risks that they don't take. What if you could have thrown the pass hurriedly in a tight window and your receiver catches it, breaks a tackle and goes for a 77 yard TD reception? You'll never know unless you actually make the throw. If you chose A, B or C – that outcome, an unlikely but possible TD, is impossible.

The key is that you are prepared to make the decision before the situation occurs. You're so conditioned to perform in such a manner over a long period of time that you understand Option A – throw the ball away, is probably the best option over the long haul – and nobody will question your judgment if you make consistent good decisions over and over again.

There are other QB attributes that can help a quarterback be successful. However, the "Decision Making" card – is the TRUMP! If you can make good decisions, all the time, your chances for success and winning the starting job dramatically improve.

Remember, there are 10 other guys in the huddle that are relying on you to make good decisions all the time. Is it right to audible to a pass play in this situation when the defense is over aggressive? Can I switch the side of our run play if the defense is over stacked to where we're running?

** THE BEST WAY TO MAKE GOOD DECISIONS IS TO PRACTICE **

If you make a bad decision in practice, it's ok. That's why it's practice. If you make a bad decision in a football game, you have to live with that consequence forever.

2 – ACCURACY

Accuracy is the #2 most important attribute for a QB. A perfect pass beats perfect coverage – every time. There is nothing more frustrating to a defensive player than running stride for stride with an offensive player and reaching up to tip a pass only to watch it gently land in a receivers hands for a completion. It's aggravating. It's demoralizing. And if you're a dominant QB – you MUST BE ACCURATE.

How can you improve your accuracy?

Be in strong position at your release point – every time. Have you ever watched a successful bowler – or a 95% free throw shooter? They have one thing in common – they perform the same motion over and over and over until it becomes routine.

I remember Michael Jordan closing his eyes and making a free throw – in a game. Why did he do it? He had practiced free throws so many times that it was second nature to him – as natural as breathing.

If you, as a QB, can get to that same point with practicing your mechanics and your delivery techniques – your accuracy ratio and completion percentage will dramatically increase!

If you want to make your team extremely happy, especially your coaching staff, improve from a 50% completion passer to a 70% completion passer. I don't know many 70% completion percentage quarterbacks who are not starters!

When you have time, watch Drew Brees in action. He throws as accurately and timely as any quarterback whoever played the game. If you want to get to that point of excellence, you have to be willing to practice, practice, practice!

There is NO SUBSTITUTE for ACCURACY!

3 – TOUGHNESS

Are you tough? I mean, can you throw a pass and get hit right between the ribs as your extended on a pass and come back from it? Can you scramble outside the pocket and dive for a 1st down while taking a big hit from a defender? Can you have enough mental fortitude to take a late hit and not be "gun shy" the next time your coach calls a pass play?

Those scenarios listed above are all predicated on physical toughness. And that's important – it's imperative that QB's are physically tough – but the physical toughness PALES IN COMPARISON to the mental toughness that it takes to play the position.

How are you going to respond to the mouthy wide receiver who comes back to the huddle and says, "DUDE, I was wide open – why didn't you throw it to me?" – right after you throw a 12 yard completion to another receiver for a 1st down? How are you going to respond? Are you going to be a hot head and yell back at your receiver? Are you going to laugh and chuckle and "brush it off"? The way you react to high stress situations is a from of toughness… and the great ones are EXTREMELY tough.

If you're not at your peak physically – you can't take the hits and the grind of football and you won't last long.

If you're not at your peak mentally – you probably won't ever set foot on the field as a starter because you will not have earned the respect of your teammates and coaches.

Making good decisions and being accurate in crunch time are all signs of "toughness."

T – Temperate
O – Opportunistic
U – Unity
G – Gamer
H – Humility

Temperate when the momentum is against you. Opportunistic when your time to play arrives. Unity and cohesiveness with your teammates and coaches. Gamer – always ready for the next challenge. Humility – never boasting of arrogance or cockiness.

That's how to be T – O – U – G – H!

4 - FOOTWORK

People used to say that Joe Montana was like a ballerina in the pocket. He would glide so smooth – like an eagle floating in the wind. And it all started with his feet. Remember, Joe Montana was an undersized – or so the critics said – scrawny kid that wasn't strong enough to play. He ended up being one of the all-time greatest... what got him to that high level? FOOTWORK.

Footwork leads to high accuracy. It's like the steering wheel in a car. If you don't have a steering wheel you're likely to veer off the road and crash. If you don't have proper footwork, you're likely to throw late and have poor results – including lots of interceptions.

Practice your footwork on a DAILY BASIS. The QB BIBLE has offered you plenty of drills to improve your footwork – perform them daily. Make it a part of your practice routine. Have your coach implement these drills on a daily basis. When your footwork improves, your game improves – and when your game improves, YOU WIN!

QB Legend Steve Young was asked once what made him such an accurate passer – his answer was short and succinct, "Footwork." That sums it up!

If you ever find yourself struggling at your quarterback play, take a peak at your footwork and notice when you have an extra hitch in your drop or when you had a false step… a successful throw starts from the waist down.

NEVER NEGLECT YOUR FOOTWORK

5 – LEADERSHIP

Go google the word "leadership" and you will find MILLIONS of search results on the subject. To some, leadership can't be explained – you either have it or you don't.

I disagree with that premise. Leadership is a skill that can be taught – just like learning how to throw a 5 step curl route. But, just like anything else, leadership takes practice.

Ask yourself these questions:

- Am I on time?
- Do I keep my word?
- How do I treat others?
- Do I strive to improve – and help others improve daily?

Those 4 simple questions can tell a person TONS about his/her leadership qualities. A person who is constantly late is not a leader. A person who says he'll do the dishes after dinner and then leaves the dishes for someone else to do is not a leader. A person who bullies or harasses another is not a leader. A person who is apathetic and stale is not a leader.

The best dominant QB's are also the best dominant leaders. They are "SHOW ME" kind of guys. They understand that talk is cheap and actions always speak louder than words. They don't need to feel a sense of entitlement over another.

True leadership is having ability to lead others. Leaders step outside themselves and are more in tune with the WHOLE rather than the PART.

If you're not a good leader, you're probably not going to be a good quarterback. You can practice leadership skills by simply improving on those 4 questions listed above.

If you're concerned that leadership may not be one of your strengths, I would suggest that you look up leadership quotes and keep them posted in visible places where you can look at them daily.

" "*A leader is one who knows the way, goes the way, and shows the way.*"

— John C. Maxwell

6 – ARM STRENGTH

Brett Favre, one of the all-time greatest QB's in the history of football, had a powerful arm. He could throw a 70 yard bomb that barely went higher than 10 feet threw the trajectory of the throw. He could ZZZZZING it! That arm strength was one of his strongest attributes – but it was also one of his biggest weaknesses.

Scouts and coaches "oooh" and "aaaaah" when they see a QB with a powerful arm that can really sling the ball. They see a physical tool that is a gift – after all, if a QB can get a pass from Point A to Point B in a faster period than another QB can in the same circumstance, it is more likely that the stronger arm will result in a more favorable play.

Arm strength is a powerful attribute...... but it MUST be tempered with the 5 characteristics listed above – especially footwork. Otherwise a quarterback with a powerful arm can take higher risks that ultimately lead to failure. Remember when Brett Favre threw a laser pass across his body in the 4th quarter of the NFC Championship game with the New Orleans Saints that was intercepted? Arm strength can be a blessing or a curse... depending on how you use it.

If you are a quarterback with average arm strength, don't fret! There are multiple ways you can increase your velocity on the football – and it doesn't all have to be bulking up in the weight room.

If you fall into the "sub par arm strength" category, focus on your footwork and decision making and the arm strength issue will be less and less of a factor – especially if you're playing mistake and turnover free football!

In Major League Baseball, they have a variety of different types of pitchers. Some are "power pitchers" that can throw 100+ miles per hour. Some are "accuracy pitchers" that can hit within inches of the catchers target – everytime. Some are "change up" pitchers who have a variety of goofy pitches that throw a batter off his rhythm. Each one of these types of pitchers are effective.

Good quarterbacks are the same way – they don't all have to be "power pitchers." However, if you can combine power, accuracy and change up – whew! – you have an advantage over your counterparts.

Arm strength is a powerful QB attribute. Perfect repetition form will lead to an increase in arm strength. Practice throwing over and over and over and over again.

7 – COOL, CALM & COLLECTED

Do you have the 3 "c's" – are you cool, calm and collected? The 3 c's help dominant QB's avoid the pressure cooker of opposing defenses. The 3 c's also play right into a quarterback's leadership abilities.

Are you cool with others when tempers flare and emotions run high towards you? Are you calm in the face of blitzing defenses? Can you keep your composure and remain collected when your receiver drops a wide open touchdown pass?

One of my favorite players to watch in the NFL now is Tom Brady. He is so cool in the pocket. He can stand there and watch 6'6 – 320 monster defensive lineman swirl around his 3' foot halo radius and keep his eyes down field the whole time.

A QB who can remain calm in the face of the storm is typically a dominant one.

How calm are you? Are you so calm that you can fall asleep in the locker room at half time? That might be a bit overboard – but the point is that in the game of football, there is NEVER ROOM FOR PANIC – in any situation, ever. Panic is the opposite of calm. Panic leads to penalties, turnovers and ultimately a loss of confidence from your teammates. Panic = BAD. Calm = GOOD.

Being collected – or having composure – is an attribute that falls in line with being cool and calm. Ok, so your receiver just dropped a wide open pass – what's the next play and how am I going to execute it? What's the situation we're in now and how are we going to respond? A dominant QB will always be under control and has composure on his side.

The "3 c's" – Cool, Calm & Collected are key ingredients in leadership – and ultimately key ingredients for winning the starting job.

ALWAYS PERFORM WITH THE 3 C's IN MIND

8 – MISTAKE FREE

Mistake free football is winning football. Often times, especially when teams are close in talent levels, the team that wins is the team that doesn't have the costly mistakes. Can you play a football game without throwing an interception? What about not taking any sacks? Did you botch a center exchange? Did you fumble a handoff?

Turnovers are huge momentum changers and lead to a sense of confidence in the opposing team. Why do you think coaches harp on the same string over and over again... how many times have you heard, "We can NOT turn the ball over."

Dominant QB's protect the football. Possession of the football is valuable. A team can not score points if they don't have the ball! Protect the football like your life depends on it – in football, your football life literally DOES depend on it.

Imagine this scenario:

Little Jonny has the strongest arm and he's such an accurate passer. In fact, he just threw for over 400 yards and 4 touchdowns in his game last week. His statistics are unbelievable – but his team lost 35-28. And why did they lose? Well – little Jonny threw 6 interceptions and had a fumbled snap. Because of those 7 turnovers his team had to play from behind the whole game and finally time ran out as they ran out of opportunities to win the game.

Those mistakes cost Little Jonny and his team an otherwise earned victory. How does his teammates and coaches feel about Jonny now? Are they as confident in him as they would be if he did not make those mistakes?

Nothing can lose a football game faster for a team than making mistakes – whether they are turnovers, penalties, poor play calling – whatever it is.

Dominant QB's minimize their mistakes. Mistake free football is winning football.

9 - COACH'S TRUST

How many times have I heard a whining athlete say to me, "Coach won't give me any playing time." Or "How come I can't get in the game?" – let me just let the cat out of the bag quickly – that player does NOT have the Coach's Trust.

If you were to tell your Mom, "Mom, I will cut the lawn this Saturday at 10 a.m." and then you come back a week later and say, "Mom, sorry I forgot to cut the lawn, I'll do it next week." And the same pattern of behavior repeats itself over and over – have you earned your Mom's trust? HECK NO!

The same condition applies in football with the coaches. If you say you want to throw a certain type of pass route and then you turn around and throw an interception, do you think your coach is going to trust you or your judgment? HECK NO!

Trust is earned by consistently and continually performing your job responsibility. You don't have to be Superman every single play... that's not your job. And, if you try to make the impossible pass, or throw the untimely throw – you're losing trust. Without trust, you have no leadership. If you have no leadership, you're more than likely sitting on the bench complaining. If you're complaining, you're trust decreases even more until the point where you literally are creating your own oblivion.

The best way to earn a coach's trust is to do what you say you're going to do, when you're going to do it. It's the same way in any relationship in your life. You didn't become best friends with someone because you simply wanted to – at some point in time you trust that person – and vice versa. You can develop a Coach's Trust by simply performing the way he/she asks you to perform consistently.

Trust in yourself. Trust in your teammates. Do your job consistently. Do those 3 things and ultimately, you will have your coach's trust. And that trust, is what separates those who start and those who ride the bench.

10 – ARE YOU HAVING FUN?!?!

Football is FUN! Where else can you line up from an opposing player and have 11 defensive players barking at you about how they're going to "rip your head off" or "tackle you so hard you cry" and you can cause just as much grief and havoc on them by simply lofting a long touchdown pass under duress in the pocket?

Where else can you get hit so hard that you can't breath and then be lifted up by an offensive lineman with a grimace on his face as he says, "I'm so sorry I got you smashed back there." And then goes out to pancake the defender on the very next running play?

The football field is where FUN happens! You can not get the same experiences you get on the football field any where else. You can't get it on a baseball diamond – where's the contact there? You can't get it on a basketball court – nobody wears helmets playing basketball. You can't get it playing golf – do you see 11 fight club guys charging Tiger Woods as he's about to tee off?

Only in the sport of football – the greatest sport in the world – can you have the hair raising, heart pumping, adrenaline flowing fun that you simply can not find any where else on earth.

Football is the game of warriors. Football is the game of true competitors. It's a game of emotion. It's a game of passion. It's a game of competitive desire. It's a game of life!

Have FUN! Smile. Enjoy the journey. Enjoy each time you get to practice. Enjoy each time you get to strap on the helmet and perform in front of hundreds of fans. Enjoy each time you get to challenge yourself to new levels of competition you never thought you would rise to. Enjoy each time you get bone crunched. Enjoy each time you execute the perfect pass with precision.

Life is full of moments and opportunities. Life is supposed to be fun. So is football! If you're not having fun…. You're not doing it right!

About the Author

Charlie Peterson was born on May 16, 1977 in San Jose, California. He was raised in South Jordan, Utah with his 6 brothers and 3 sisters.

Charlie's list of football accomplishments include:

- Utah USA TODAY Player of the Year – Bingham High School – 1995

- Full ride scholarship to Brigham Young University - 1996 – 2002

- Former BYU starting QB - 2000 - 2002
    1. Threw for over 2,000 yards and 10 touchdowns in career at BYU
    2. Played under legendary college football coach Lavell Edwards
    3. Played under offensive coordinator Norm Chow & Gary Crowton

- Threw for over 4,000 yards and 120 touchdowns in the Arena Football League

- Played professional football in Canada with the Toronto Argonauts

- Has thrown for over 10,000 yards and 100 touchdowns in the semi-pro RMFL

He is married to the love of his life, Danielle.

Charlie can be reached via email at
chuckypita@gmail.com

Made in the USA
Lexington, KY
02 December 2017